M000016966

From:

PUSH!

Pray Until Something Happens

Written and compiled by Sarah M. Hupp
Design by Heather Zschock

INSPIRE

Inspire Books is an imprint
of Peter Pauper Press, Inc.

For permissions, please see the
last page of this book.

Copyright © 2000
Peter Pauper Press, Inc.
202 Mamaroneck Avenue
White Plains, NY 10601
All rights reserved
ISBN 0-88088-140-2
Printed in China
14   13   12   11   10   9

Visit us at www.peterpauper.com

PUSH!

Pray Until Something Happens

We live in an instant society.

Minute Rice®.
Instant pudding.
Microwaveable meals.

We expect instant results—and that goes for spiritual things too. We expect our prayers to rattle the cage of heaven and bring immediate results. When those results don't come quickly enough, we get discouraged or lose interest in bringing even the simplest requests to God.

Our instant spirits need a dose of perseverance! Daniel's persistence in prayer brought an angelic visitor who reminded Daniel that as soon as he began to pray "an answer was given" (Daniel 9:23, NIV). God has already heard your prayers too. May this little book bring you encouraging reminders to press on and

Pray Until Something Happens.

S. M. H.

No man can be the ULTIMATE
without the strength of a
HIGHER SOURCE.
That source comes from
GOD IN CHRIST. If it is God's
will, NO MAN NOR POWER
ON EARTH CAN STOP ME.

BOBBY BOWDEN

In prayer we set aside
our agendas, letting
GOD'S PRIORITIES become
our priorities, and we
RECEIVE HIS RESOURCES.

JOHN F. WESTFALL

Continue earnestly in prayer, being vigilant in it with thanksgiving.

COLOSSIANS 4:2, NJKV

Ask and it will be given to you;
seek and you
will find;
knock and the door will
be opened to you.
For everyone who asks receives;
he who seeks finds;
and to him who knocks,
the door will be opened.

MATTHEW 7:7-8 NIV

Our hope depends not on the right technique or the proper phrase or gesture, which borders on magic, but on the promises of God to look with favor on those who throw themselves on his mercy.

DONALD BLOESCH

Each of us may be sure that if God sends us over rocky paths, He will provide us with *sturdy shoes*. He will never send us on any journey without equipping us well.

ALEXANDER MACLAREN

Every difficulty that presents itself to us, if we receive it in the right way, is God's opportunity.

C. H. PARKHURST

I CAN DO ALL THINGS
THROUGH CHRIST WHICH
STRENGTHENETH ME.

PHILIPPIANS 4:13 KJV

[W]E HAVE confidence BEFORE GOD; AND WHATEVER WE ASK WE RECEIVE FROM HIM, BECAUSE WE KEEP HIS COMMANDMENTS AND DO THE THINGS THAT ARE PLEASING IN HIS SIGHT.

1 JOHN 3:21–22 NASB

Satan may build a hedge about us and fence us in and hinder our movements, but he cannot roof us in and prevent our looking up.

J. HUDSON TAYLOR

Trust GOD'S PROMISES
WHEN PRAYER'S ANSWERS
TARRY. ANSWERS ALWAYS
COME BY THE PATHS OF
GOD'S promises.

TRUST

God's Promises

Drop Thy still dews
  of quietness,
Till all our strivings cease;
Take from our souls
  the strain and stress,
And let our ordered
  lives confess
The beauty of Thy peace.

JOHN G. WHITTIER

When circumstances are
against us, we must be able
to set the sails of our souls
and use even adverse winds.

E. STANLEY JONES

He knows the way I take;
When He has tried me,
I shall come forth as gold.

JOB 23:10 NASB

[N]ot only can I trust the hand that lights the fire, I can also have the assurance the fire will not consume but only refine. And when the refining process is complete, not a moment too soon or too late, "I will come forth as gold." (Job 23:10).

J. R. MACDUFF

Extraordinary afflictions
are not always the
punishment of
extraordinary sins,
but sometimes the trial of
extraordinary graces.

MATTHEW HENRY

Why are you cast down,

O my soul? And why are you

disquieted within me?

Hope in God;

For I shall yet praise Him, The help

of my countenance and my God.

PSALMS 42:11 NKJV

Go *boldly* to God. He desires your prayers and has commanded you to *pray*. He promises to hear you, not because you are good but because he is good.

WILLIAM TYNDALE

Whenever God gives us a cross to bear, he has also given us a PROMISE that he will give us the STRENGTH to bear it.

The LORD will give STRENGTH unto his people; the LORD will bless his people with PEACE.

PSALMS 29:11 KJV

OUR **Lord's lessons**
AND EXAMPLES TEACH US THAT
PRAYER THAT IS NOT STEADFAST
AND PERSISTENT, NOR REVIVED
AND REFRESHED, AND DOES
NOT GATHER STRENGTH FROM
PREVIOUS PRAYERS IS NOT THE
PRAYER THAT WILL TRIUMPH.

WILLIAM ARTHUR

Cast your burden upon the LORD, and He will sustain you; He will never allow the righteous to be shaken.

PSALMS 55:22 NASB

The stops of a good man are ordered by the Lord as well as his steps.

GEORGE MÜLLER

ART THOU WEARY, TENDER HEART?

BE GLAD OF PAIN!

In sorrow sweetest
things will grow,

AS FLOWERS IN RAIN.

GOD WATCHES;

THOU WILT HAVE THE SUN,

WHEN CLOUDS THEIR PERFECT

WORK HAVE DONE.

ADELAIDE PROCTER

If you PRAY FOR BREAD and bring no basket to carry it, you prove the doubting spirit which may be the only hindrance to the gift you ask.

DWIGHT L. MOODY

[W]eeping may endure

for a night, but

JOY COMETH IN THE MORNING.

PSALMS 30:5 KJV

The soul would have no rainbow

Had the eyes no tears.

JOHN V. CHENEY

RESHAPE!

RECREATE!

RENEW!

REMOLD!

RESTORE!

Redeem

The vicissitudes of life often leave us cracked and broken! If we are willing to be remolded, reshaped, renewed, restored, re-created, and even redeemed by a loving, caring, compassionate, and empathetic Potter we too may come forth as wondrous and awesome people.

JOCELYN M. ROPER

You will keep him
in perfect peace,
Whose mind is stayed
on You, Because he
trusts in You.

ISAIAH 26:3 NKJV

God is the universal
dispeller of all gloom,
and the glorious dispenser
of all gladness in the soul.

B. M'CALL BARBOUR

It is the end that
crowns us,
not the fight.

ROBERT HERRICK

[T]he joy of the LORD
is your strength.

NEHEMIAH 8:10 KJV

[T]he ability to find joy in life really is a tremendous strength. The people who can... delight in the joy of the moment are going to live a lot longer than [those] of us who are stressed and pushed and taking ourselves terribly seriously.

CLAIRE CLONINGER

Joy removes difficulties. Joy is to our service as oil is to the wheels of a railroad car. Without oil the axle grows hot and accidents occur. If there is no holy joy to oil our wheels, our spirit will soon be clogged with weariness.

CHARLES H. SPURGEON

We look not at the things which are seen, but at the things which are not seen; for the things which are seen are temporal, but the things which are not seen are eternal.

2 CORINTHIANS 4:18 NASB

God calls us into the eye
of the storms of our lives.
The storms will come.
They will come strong

Calm

Peace

with great rage. But, in the midst of the fury is the eye where we find complete calm and peace.

SANDRA L. SWANS

Afflictions are but
the shadows of God's
wings.

GEORGE MACDONALD

With a surrendered attitude, I can bring my requests to God. I don't have to tell God what to do. Instead, I watch, wait and cooperate. To accept God's sovereignty is one more necessary surrender.

JAN JOHNSON

The LORD your God is with you, he is mighty to save. He will take great delight in you, he will quiet you with his love.

ZEPHANIAH 3:17 NIV

Will prayers that do
not move the heart of
the supplicant move
the heart of the
Omnipotent?

Come to me, all you who are weary and burdened, and I will give you rest.

MATTHEW 11:28 NIV

God does not dispense strength and encouragement like a druggist fills your prescription. The Lord doesn't promise to give us something to take so we can handle our weary moments. **He promises us Himself.** That is all. And that is enough.

CHARLES W. SWINDOLL

OUR SIGHT MAY BRING DISCOURAGING REPORTS ABOUT PRAYER'S EFFECTIVENESS. PAY NO ATTENTION TO IT. God is still in control. EVEN THE DELAY TO THE ANSWER OF OUR PRAYERS IS PART OF HIS GOOD PLAN.

If the sun of God's countenance shine upon me, I may well be content to be wet with the rain of affliction.

JOSEPH HALL

Sometimes a light surprises
The Christian while he sings;
It is the Lord who rises
With healing in His wings:
When comforts are declining
He grants the soul again
A season of clear shining
To cheer it after rain.

WILLIAM COWPER

SING SING SING SING SING SING SING SING SING SING SING SING SING SING SING

cheer!

[T]HEY THAT WAIT UPON THE LORD
SHALL RENEW THEIR STRENGTH;
THEY SHALL MOUNT UP WITH WINGS
AS EAGLES; THEY SHALL RUN, AND
NOT BE WEARY; AND THEY SHALL
WALK, AND NOT FAINT.

ISAIAH 40:31 KJV

Iron till it be thoroughly heated is incapable to be wrought; so God sees good to cast some men into the furnace of affliction, and then beats them on his anvil into what frame he pleases.

ANNE BRADSTREET

IF YOU ABANDON YOURSELF
TO GOD, YOU WILL NEVER BE
ABANDONED BY GOD.

BE OF GOOD courage,
AND HE SHALL STRENGTHEN
YOUR HEART, ALL YOU WHO
HOPE IN THE LORD.

PSALMS 31:24 NKJV

TOO SOON WE CEASE OUR STRIVING IN PRAYER. WHEN ANSWERS TARRY, WE GIVE UP. THIS IS A DEADLY MISTAKE THAT FRAMES THE WAY OF FAILURE. WE MUST PRAY UNTIL WHAT WE PRAY FOR IS ACCOMPLISHED OR UNTIL WE ARE ASSURED THAT IT WILL BE.

[W]e must allow God the freedom to work in our souls in whatever way He pleases, knowing that He is an accomplished Master and will produce in us a masterpiece.

JOSEPH GIRZONE

The LORD'S LOVING KINDNESSES
indeed never cease, For His
compassions never fail.
They are new every morning;
Great is Thy faithfulness.

LAMENTATIONS 3:22–23 NASB

[E]ach day is new,
yesterday is gone,
and God is the God
of a second chance.
Though others may
fail and disappoint,
He never will.

RUTH GRAHAM DIENERT

Troubles are often
the tools by which
God fashions us for
better things.

HENRY WARD BEECHER

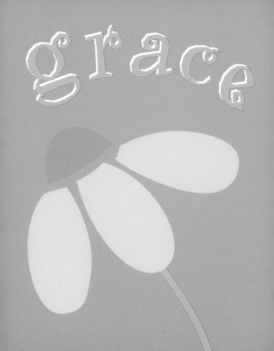

God, who gives all grace, will make everything right. He will make you strong and support you and keep you from falling.

1 PETER 5:10 NCV

Thou art coming to a King,
Large petitions with
you bring;
For his grace and
power are such
None can ever ask
too much.

JOHN NEWTON

In the spiritual realm, adversity signifies advance. If there are no problems, no tensions, no uncertainties, things are not functioning according to the biblical norm.... [T]he higher you set your goals, the greater the pressure you'll experience.

MIKE PHILLIPS

The LORD is my light
and my salvation;
Whom shall I fear?
The LORD is the
strength of my life;
Of whom shall I
be afraid?

PSALMS 27:1 NKJV

When you walk with the assurance that the **Lord is your light and salvation,** then you need to fear no thing and no one. God places sweet peace and quietness within our reach.... God soothes our anxieties, calms our mistrusts, settles our upsets. Our God is all-powerful.

LILLIAN HARRIS CARTER

All occasions invite His mercies, and all times are His seasons.

GEORGE HERBERT

WHENEVER I AM AFRAID,
I WILL TRUST IN YOU.

PSALMS 56:3 NKJV

As we go out to face whatever
is before us, may we do so
with the courage and patience
and hope born of the knowledge
that we are His, and that
He is ours, through faith in the
once crucified, but now
glorified, Redeemer.

JAMES M. GRAY

Easy paths without fit the pilgrim for exhausting climb up

sharp stones never

the steep, rough,

the "hill of difficulty."

M. TAYLOR

[W]e can be certain that God will surround us with his protection. He will send *angels* to battle our enemy and a pillar of fire to brighten our darkness. Though evil may threaten us, it will never overwhelm us.

ANN SPANGLER

You keep your LOVING
PROMISE and lead the
people you have saved.
With your STRENGTH you
will guide them to
your holy place.

EXODUS 15:13 NCV

The feeble hands and helpless

Groping out into the darkness

Touch God's right hand
in that darkness,

And are lifted up
and strengthened.

HENRY WADSWORTH LONGFELLOW

Being a Christian is no excuse for mediocrity or passive acceptance of defeat. If anything, Christianity demands a higher standard, even more devotion to the task.

OREL HERSHISER

Delight yourself in the Lord and he will give you the desires of your heart.

PSALMS 37:4 NIV

Where there is quiet and meditation, there is neither care nor waste.
Where there is compassion and discretion, there is neither excess nor indifference.
Where the fear of the Lord guards the door, the enemy cannot enter.

ST. FRANCIS OF ASSISI

[I]n due time we shall reap if we do not grow weary.

GALATIANS 6:9 NASB

Once you have handed the
matter over to God . . .
you must dare to believe
that He has taken it in hand
and that, though He may
keep you waiting, He will
not be at rest until
He has finished it.

F. B. MEYER

CLOCKS NEED WINDING, CLEANING, AND OILING. SOMETIMES THEY NEED REPAIR. SIMILARLY, WE MUST CARE FOR OUR SPIRITUAL LIFE BY EXAMINING AND SERVICING OUR HEARTS... KEEP YOUR EYES ON HEAVEN. DON'T THROW IT AWAY FOR EARTHLY THINGS. LOOK AT JESUS CHRIST AND BE FAITHFUL TO HIM.

FRANCIS DE SALES

Be joyful always;
pray continually;
give thanks in all
circumstances, for this
is God's will for you...

1 THESSALONIANS 5:16–18 NIV